LOOK WHO'S HERE!

By
Bil Keane

FAWCETT GOLD MEDAL • NEW YORK

A Fawcett Gold Medal Book

Published by Ballantine Books

Copyright © 1960, 1970 by The Register & Tribune Syndicate, Inc.

Copyright © 1972 by CBS Publications, The Consumer Publishing Division of CBS, Inc.

ISBN 0-449-13276-5

Printed in the U.S.A.

First Fawcett Gold Medal Edition: March 1972
First Canadian Edition: April 1983
First Ballantine Books Edition: April 1983
Twenty-fourth printing: July 1987

"You used to WORK before you were married,
didn't you, Mommy?"

"See? I'm ALMOST your age!"

"Why do I have to wash the BACKS of my hands?
I only eat with the FRONTS!"

"Why do we only use the tablecloth Grandma
gave us when she's here for dinner?"

"Mommy, can you itch my back 'cause
it scratches."

"I forgot. Today's Show and Tell!"

"I have to write 50 facts for tomorrow. What's a fact?"

"Mommy smells like she's going someplace."

"Once upon a time there lived a very beautiful
little fairy princess..."

"Miss Helen said if I'm walking at night I have
to wear white and if I'm not wearing any
clothes I should wave a hanky "

"It's going to rain! We heard the sky mumbling."

"Do I hafta come in? It's just drizzling!"

"Don't just kiss it! Put something on it!"

"Who won, Billy?"

"Okay, I drew the doggy, and the horsey, and
the bunny rabbit, and the daddy reading
and the little boy asleep...NOW
what do you want me to draw?"

"But this is the best house anybody ever built! It doesn't leak much an' it feels GOOD in here!"

"Somebody must've TOLD Barfy we're going on vacation without him!"

"Is it MY turn to sit in the front-seat, yet?"

"No, we're not almost there. We've gone 35 miles
and Grandma's house is still 465 miles away."

"I woke PJ up so he can help us watch for deer!"

"Not that one! Their pool doesn't have a slid-
ing board!"

"They have a kiddie pool and a game room and
soda machines and swings and a pool table and
ping-pong...which are we going to do first?"

"Why aren't you wearing this pretty lace nightie
of yours, Mommy?"

"You just THINK you do, Jeffy. Let's all sing
a little song."

"NOW I 'member where my bathing suit is! Is it
very far back to the railing outside the motel
we stayed at last night?"

"Couldn't I have a grilled cheese sandwich?"

"We turn off at that splash of mustard, then a few miles past the chocolate spot, we bear right to just beyond the catsup."

"If we don't look very good to you, Grandma,
it's because we've been traveling a lot."

"After you show us your flowers, Grandma, then
can you show us your 'frigerator?"

"Look! Grandma's using the pencil holder I made her, and the paperweight I made, and there's Billy's handprint in plaster, and..."

"Here's an open spot! PJ might fall out here!"

"Don't you have any little kids around here for
us to play with, Grandma?"

"Lollipops? Sugar cereal? Comic books? Animal crackers? Kiddie bath? Are you sure this is your cart, Mrs. Carne?"

"Gee, Mommy, I wish you had a dresser drawer full of neat stuff like Grandma's."

"At our house Mommy always hides the candy on the top shelf."

"Hey! Look at Grandma's toothpaste! Folded
up nice and neat!"

"After the three gen'rations of girls, let's take a picture of the FIVE gen'rations of BOYS!"

"This just came in the mail for you. It says,
'Having nice time, wish you were here,
Love, Billy, Dolly, Jeffy and PJ!'"

"Are you SURE you can't come home with us?
There's still some room!"

"See, PJ? There's the shopping center--and
doesn't that bridge look familiar? And this hill?
NOW do you know where we are?"

"Come on, Barfy, into the c. . ."

"The trouble with comin' home from vacation is
there's never anything to do."

"We hit a lot of bugs, Daddy! Why didn't you stop for them?"

"When we were on vacation at Grandma Carne's
we. . ."
"Then Grandma Carne baked a. . ."
"And Grandma Carne took us to a. . ."

"I'm going to wash the ice cream off my hands."

"Boy! You sure don't know how to use
your manners!"

"Today's the day I take care of my garden. I.
have to water my carrot."

"My carrot isn't done yet so I put it back in the ground."

"Mommy, how do these feel on me?"

"Relax! That's just a 'cookie will cure it' cry."

"This is far enough, Mommy! We can walk the
rest of the way to the bus stop by ourselves!"

"I better give you another kiss 'cause you just
wiped that other one off."

"Do they use these box tops again, Mommy? Is that why they want them?"

"If you think this is noisy, Grandma, you should
be inside our school bus!"

"It's okay, Daddy--they're brothers!"

"Know where Mommy used to live? In GRANDMA'S house!"

"Are you sure one cookie will fill you up?"

"Billy? Did you hear that same funny noise in
your dream that I heard in mine?"

"Dolly, get the egg beater out of the bathtub;
Jeffy, bring me the measuring spoons from the
sandbox; Billy, those minnows will have
to move out of the mixing bowl..."

"They said I had Mommy's nose and Daddy's hair
and Grandma's eyes....I thought I looked like ME!"

"Mommy, can you hit some to us, now?".

"To your right. . . .your RIGHT! The hand you
eat with. . .now, back this way. . ."

"Would you please just bring it around to
the gate?"

"Why does Mommy always say 'Have a good day'?
She KNOWS we're going to SCHOOL!"

"I was playin' in LOTS of yards--Wilseys',
Littles', Allens', Reeds'. . . .I don't
know where I left my jacket!"

"Mommy...I mean, Miss Helen!..."

"Red Rover, Red Rover for HOT PINK to come over!
Red Rover, Red Rover for AVOCADO to come over...!"

"You don't have to bother cookin' dinner,
Mommy. We picked up pizzas!"

"Daddy, would you buy me Super City for
my birthday, but I won't go with you
'cause I want to be surprised."

"I think Billy's birthday present better be something FOUR can play with."

"Don't forget what day tomorrow is, Mommy!"

"Mommy! Jeffy didn't say 'Happy Birthday' to me."

"Billy, give me the answer to number five. . .
Billy!. . .Billy?. . ."

"Gee, I'm lucky—I gotta Grandma an' Grandpa—an' I'm only 7."

"Oh boy! That's just what I was HOPIN'
you'd get!"

"I know the punch line to that one, Daddy: The
man said, 'I wouldn't turn a knight out
on a dog like this!' Right?"

"...93, 94, 95... Grandma said to get something
I wanted with the dollar... 96, 97..."

"Do I have to have dinner tonight? We had
cupcakes, cookies, candy, popcorn and
somethin' purple to drink at our party."

"But we didn't go to Thompsons' yet or the Daniels'
--and we didn't do any of Woodland Road or
those houses by the railroad, and..."

"You may eat ONE thing!"

"Mrs. Klink says can we play inside today 'cause
the real estate man is bringing some
people to look at her house."

"Except for a brief bathtub scene starring PJ,
this picture has been rated 'G'."

"Wonder when they're going to unpack their kids."

"Wow! Those new people came from Texas and
Alabama and North Carolina and Illinois
and Vermont and..."

"Mommy! The people movin' in next door have
a little child! Can we go over there to play?"

"You have a gray hair, Daddy. Does that mean
you're going to be a granddad soon?"

"Mommy, is this a hat to sing 'Happy Birthday' in,
or do you wear it to yell 'Happy New Year'?"

"We better not fight 'cause there might be something on TV tonight we want to watch!"

"Aw, Mommy! He's warming up the bed for me!"

"Wait, mailman, wait!"

"Mommy! Know who I wish our Daddy was?"

"Santa Claus sees you."

"It would be more fun lookin' at Mommy's present
if we hadn't had it gift wrapped."

"What's going on down here?"

"...And please make the days go FASTER."

"How's it look, Daddy?"

"Can we open the ones that say 'And Children'?"

"Did Santa leave a guarantee with this?"

"His daddy won't let him play 'em at his house.
Can he play 'em over here?"

"Why do I have to write a thank you note to Grandma? She only gave us CLOTHES!"

"Mommy! I came untucked!"

"Aw--you mean that's the prize for straightening
up our room? Just a kiss?"

"Couldn't we leave it up 'til Grandma and
Granddad come to see us next summer?"

"Jack Frost did so paint the pretty pictures on the window, didn't he, Daddy?"

"How'd you manage to get all this cereal in here?"

"Man! I'd hate to be a banker. I'm having an
awful time counting these pennies."

"Jennifer and Rita shouldn't even BE in kinder-
garten 'cause they don't know how to button yet."

"Watch me count! 1, 2, 3, 4, 5, 6, 7, 8, 9, 10—
and I've got 11 and 12 but I don't know where
to put 'em!"

"Look at this, Jeffy! Clovers on every card!"

"Can you open the door so Daddy can see me waving, too?"

"No, dummy! Blow OUT, not IN!"

"Did you know Mrs. Warner just washed all her windows? She told me when I put my nose against one."

"Feel my head and see if I have a headache."

"Mommy! You'd have been real proud of me.
today! I got to be cookie passer!"

"PJ crawled under the bed and got covered
with fur!"

"Well, all right. We'll keep him 'til we find
out who his owner is,"

"...And he's very shaggy and wearing no collar.
If you've lost this dog please phone us
as the people who found him are
anxious to find its owner."

"No, Sam! That's just our Daddy! He's
allowed in!"

"Hi, Grandma! Did you come to see our
new doggy?"

"Sammy! Get in here before you
get AMMONIA!"

."Stop that sneezin', Sam! I'm tired of God-blessing you."

"Dogs must really like babies. Sam and Barfy
are always hangin' around PJ's chair."

"If anybody gets spanked, it makes Sam growl!"

"I need some more destruction paper, Mommy."

"She can't come to the phone--she's in the bathtub with the plumber."